Master Shigeho Tanaka

First steps in
AIKIDO

Wendy Walker

Paul H. Crompton Ltd.
94 Felsham Road
London SW15 1DQ
England

First Edition 1997
Reprinted 1998

ISBN No 1 874250 50 2

London: Paul H.Crompton Ltd.
94 Felsham Road, Putney, London SW15 1DQ

*Printed and bound in England
by Caric Press
Clerwood, Corunna Main,
Andover, Hants SP10 IJE
(01264) 354887*

Contents

Master Tanaka's calligraphy for the syllable "En", meaning "Connections".

PREFACE

My passion for Aikido and enjoyment of teaching has lead me to write this book with the aim of enlightening those less knowledgeable and experienced than myself. I have been aided in this humble effort by my friend and instructor, Pat Stratford, 6th Dan and guided by most respected friend, Norio Tao, 6th Dan. This project has been conceived as I am lowly enough in grade and ability to empathise with beginners and kyu grades (grades below black belt), yet high enough to instruct.

So, why write a book in the first place? Beginners are always asking what books can they read. Usually the answer is there is no substitute for practice. They should be able to learn all they need to known in the training hall (dojo). The trouble is that this isn't always possible. Classes may be large, the Instructor may be able to demonstrate but not teach or explain. Sometimes you don't get all the help and guidance you need. I have seen books on Aikido which either try to teach it step by step or give high powered incomprehensible theory. This book will give you the basics in simple language. You may find some things fall into place instantly but you will need to apply the principles herein so that you are capable of studying and understanding more. This book is above all a guide and supplement to the practise of Aikido.

We all need explanations as well as physical training and instruction. This book meant to give you information and practical help. It is no use without the physical training. Knowing something is totally different to being able to do it. I have seen observers sit on the sidelines, urging others on and giving directions. If they were on the mat (tatami) they wouldn't have a clue! There is also a difference in experiencing the power of a throw or the subtlety of a move, which no amount of written instruction can give. Lastly, a book does not train and develop body and mind as does continuous practise of Aikido.

Training within a framework of knowledge is the key. Yet good Aikido may be hard to find. Some schools teach their pupils to fall for each other because they cannot do technique. Ever heard someone ask, "What's the matter? Can't you do ukemi?" (breakfall). Others may become brutal through frustration and lack of skill. Aikido is practised in a variety of ways and at different levels of competence even by Instructors of

*Master Tanaka demonstrates Aiki nage at the Shiseikan dojo,
Meiji Jingu, Tokyo.*

Pat Stratford executing Kokyu Nage.

*Pat Stratford, President and National Coach
of the Aikido Union of Great Britain.*

like grade. As you learn more you will become more aware of these differences. The intricacies of Aikido would take volumes. I have been told by the highest Dan grades that a lifetime is not long enough for a true study. All I want to do here is to help the beginner to understand what should be happening during his/her training (for the purposes of this book I shall use the male gender, apologies to the many female aikidoka), and show how he can improve.

To beginners, instructors may seem miserly with information. A little is given here and there, as he goes around the class. An instructor should know how much can be taken in at various stages of training by different individuals. Some instructors may test your determination before attempting to take you to a higher level. However I have trained with kyu grades, who were clearly in a fog. Although they were going through the motions, they had lost their way. The explanation of a few basic principles saw their Aikido improve dramatically. Imagine Aikido as a jigsaw. You must identify the simplest pieces before you can start to put the picture together with vision and application, the rest of the pieces will eventually fall into place. The picture will then shift and change as you learn more, you may even add dimensions – but it will be the same picture.

Information and explanations should help you to understand Aikido and practice Aikido. You still have a lot of studying to do but you should always try to do your thinking off the tatami so that you make full use of your training periods. Practicing on your own is a good way to consolidate your learning at the beginning. Work with an imaginary opponent and perform the basic exercises or basic techniques, reminding yourself of the names and key points as you go.

I assume that because you have picked up this book you are an enthusiastic beginner or kyu grade, dissatisfied with the information at hand. Even enthusiasts may quickly become discouraged. So often I have heard, "I love Aikido. I will never ever give it up", before the last appearance of a fellow student.

Why is it so difficult to study Aikido? Many reasons contribute. You will and must develop good coordination and flexibility of body and of mind. I will give you one picture of Aikido, learn by it, don't stick rigidly to it. You must learn to synchronise your movements. You must maintain good posture, a positive spirit even against the odds. Positive is not aggressive but determined. You must subdue your own ego to learn from others and in particular bear the admonishments of your instructor. You must have faith in yourself, your instructor and Aikido itself.

How many people can take these rigours? Very few, that is why the drop out rate in Aikido is so high. But hang on in there. Grit your teeth, subdue your pride and ego, listen and pay attention, then you'll see that anything is possible. Keep training, keep studying and those impossible throws (the ones that you don't believe anyway), they will fall into place. You'll be amazed at what you can do and all the times that you felt that you were banging your head against a brick wall will seem to fade into dim memory and be of no significance.

If you can't understand what I am talking about and think that Aikido is easy, you are either brilliant or you should take a long hard look at the training you are receiving. Do you choose to make a breakfall or do you have no choice? Do you harmonise with the attacker or does he harmonise with you? In real Aikido you tell yourself that you are not going to fall but inevitably you find yourself flying through the air again.

Just being able to do the unbelievable is one of the joys of Aikido and enough reason for us students to keep on training. Other benefits include better fitness, flexibility and coordination, more energy and a positive attitude to life. Eventually there is a feeling of completeness and peace akin to that achieved in meditation by the concentration of body and mind together and the focusing of spirit. This is Riai, the blending of truth, spirit, body and mind.

Having taught children and beginners for the last nine years, I have a good idea of the problems that you are now encountering and an appreclation of your lack of ability at this stage. I still remember vividly some of my early training experiences: the grip that felt like a vice, the blow which came towards me with terrifying speed and power. I fell into many traps because I did not have the knowledge and experience to deal with them or the necessary guidance at the time.

Having stumbled upon Aikido quite by accident, I found that I had entered a fascinating world where anything seemed possible. Logic told me that I was being ridiculous, a middle-aged woman trying to enter what seemed the male dominated area of martial arts. In my heart of hearts I knew that this was where I belonged and that nothing else in life could ever compare. Now I know that Aikido is not a martial art but an art of preparation for life. Through the practise of Aikido I have learned to listen to my inner self more and more and I believe that this is the true way.

For the last six years I have been studying directly under my friend and instructor Pat Stratford, 6th Dan, who is the founder of the Aikido Union of England and its President and National Coach. I have also studied briefly under Master Shigeho Tanaka, 9th Dan, of the Shiseiken Dojo, in the Meiji Jingu, Tokyo.

Pat Stratford has been studying Budo since his teens, when he was in the Special Forces. His first Dan grade was in Judo but when he saw Aikido, he could not believe his eyes. He searched the world to find out more and was thrown many times before he did believe!

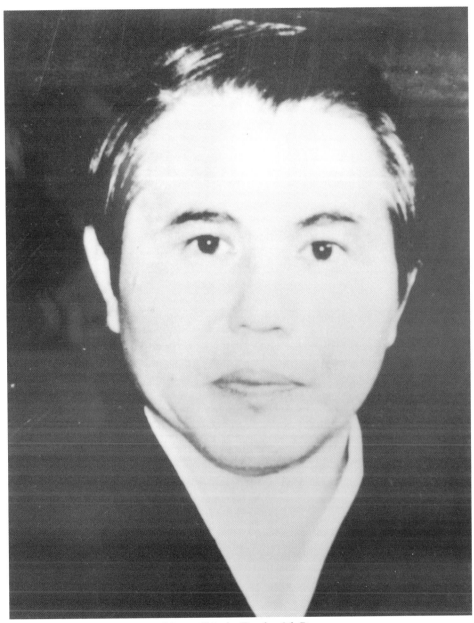

Master Shigeho Tanaka, 9th Dan.

On the Continent, he trained under Andre Nocquet, Alain Floquet, Tadashi Abe, Nobuyoshi Tamura and Mutsuro Nakazone. He learned from all these Masters but was still not satisfied until he met a man called Norio Tao. This was the Aikido for which he had been searching. Norio Tao was a highly respected student of Master Shigeho Tanaka. Through the years strong ties have been forged with Norio Tao and Master Tanaka.

Pat has been studying Aikido now for some thirty years and was one of the first to teach in England. He was offered various positions in the martial arts world but he has always preferred to follow the way of Budo. As a trained instructor of Aikido not only has he been an inspiration for all his Dan grades but he continues to amaze us year after year with his increasing power and ingenuity. His most basic precept is "absorb, deflect, project", a simple formula which applies to all techniques and which I will expand upon in Chapter 2.

Under Pat's tuition I have learned that techniques can change subtly when using a different format. They can also be developed and made more and more efficient. This means that the possibilities in Aikido are endless. We can never learn it all because Aikido stretches to infinity. In some martial arts, age means a deterioration in strength and speed, leading to a lack of effectiveness. In Aikido, age means that there has been more time to develop greater skill and power, leading to greater effectiveness.

Pat Stratford was awarded 6th Dan Aikido, 6th Dan Budo by Master Shigeho Tanaka in Tokyo, in 1986. Master Tanaka himself is a 9th Dan and a highly acclaimed Aikidoka in Japan. He studied under Morihei Ueshiba at the Hombu Dojo with Yamada and others. He also sought out and studied under other more ancient Masters. He has taught in Universities throughout Japan and Asia and performed demonstrations in Canada. In 1993, he was awarded 9th Dan and honoured by the Emperor for his service to Aikido and to Japan. He recently retired as director of the Meiji Jingu, Tokyo. He is now the honorary director and he continues to instruct there at the Shiseikan Dojo.

The Aikido Union of England has enjoyed a long association with Master Tanaka. He is a source of inspiration and is idolised as the spirit of Aikido and Budo. He visited England in 1992, with Norio Tao, Hirosuke Fujisawa and other disciples to give a course of instruction and the power of his techniques. We were awed by the positive nature of his Aikido and treated to a demonstration of the sword (Kashima shin ryu).

Last year (1993), Pat was invited to Japan by Master Tanaka and honoured for his understanding of Budo and Aikido. I was also invited to accompany him. We trained with Master Tanaka at the Shiseikan Dojo in the Meiji Jingu but a greater priority for the visit was the study of the spiritual side of Aikido in many ways. We learned a lot simply by observing the Aikidoka in Japan and how they helped each other and provided a high

Norio Tao, Pat Stratford and Master Tanaka at the Kyomi Temple, Tokyo.

Entrance to the Meiji Jingu shrine dedicated to the Emperor Maiji (1853–1912).

level of support and cooperation in other facets of their lives. We were also invited to visit the many shrines and temples in the Kyoto area and we learned about their history and their importance to Budo and Aikido.

One of the things which most impressed me was our visit to the sacred Mount Hiei and the Enryakuji Temple. This famous temple began when Saicho, at the age of eighteen, built a hut on the top of Mount Hiei and did spiritual practise there. He used the wood from a fallen tree to carve an image of Yakushi Nyorai, the Buddha of Healing and erected a small building to house the image. This temple is now the primary hall of the Enryakuji and it houses the "inextinguishable Dharma Light", which has been shining for the last twelve hundred years.

I cannot describe the atmosphere in this temple except to say that I felt deeply drawn to the shrine. Only now in writing this book do I recall that the Buddha worshipped there was the Buddha of healing and I wonder at my own practice of Shiatsu and subsequent introduction to Reiki by Reiki Master, Simon Treselyan.

Returning to the story of Saicho, he visited China to study Buddhism under many eminent priests and on his return funded the Tendai Sect. He devoted himself to the education of many who followed him. His intent was to create 'people who would illumine their surroundings." He was renamed Dengyo Daishi by the Emperor, himself. Dengyo means "great teacher, introducing Buddhism".

At this temple, Norio Tao explained to us that everyone was invited here to light a candle "to light up one corner". The meaning of this is to be a guiding light either as a teacher or as an example to the community. I lit two candles to make my "corner" brighter still.

In writing this book, I hope to illumine my surroundings and shed light on one area of Aikido, admittedly the first and simplest. If you can appreciate the basic principles which are contained here and see the picture which I am trying to present, you will start to understand Aikido. Then you will know how to study and discover the hidden wealth and wonders which await you on the tatarni.

The Shiseikan dojo, Tokyo.

Pat Stratford with a certificate of honour. Author, Hirosuke Fujisawa, Master Tanaka,

The Kinkauji – Golden Pavilion.

INTRODUCTION

Although the founder of modern Aikido is generally accepted to be Morihei Ueshiba, the origins can be traced much further back and others may well have been working along similar lines to make the Aikido of today an inevitable consequence of changes in times and attitudes.

Aiki-jujitsu is said to have been invented by Prince Teijun, a son of the Emperor Seiwa. Prince Teijun was an accomplished warrior who used empty-handed sword strokes to defeat his enemies by aiming at openings in their armour. The system was further improved and altered by his descendants so that it included the defence against various weapons. The Daito-ryu Aiki-jujitsu school was founded by one of his descendants, General Shinra Saburo Yoshimitsu, in the twelfth century AD. Daito was the name of the family estate. This school taught the use of weapons and empty-handed techniques based on the same principles.

The samurai learned their fighting skills from many such schools, each with their own techniques and different ways. Daimyo (lords) would often establish their own schools for use by their samurai and appoint a renowned swordsman as teacher. Although the samurai were paid warriors, who fought in the power struggles between the daimyo, in fact they were a servant class, tied by family loyalty to their masters, their behaviour imposed by the warriors code, Bushido.

The Bushido code was necessary to balance the power of such fighting men with duties and responsibilities. In a feudal society, the samurai were used to keep law and order and maintain the status quo. Shinto taught reverence to ancestors and loyalty to the Emperor, who was descended from the gods, but by the eighth

Master Tanaka demonstrates Batto Jutsu at the Shiseikan dojo.

century, real power began to move into the hands of a series of self appointed military dictators called shoguns. The shoguns demanded allegiance from the Daimyo, who in turn were served by their samurai. In social order, the samurai ranked above peasants, merchants and artisans. They had substantial privileges and even the right to kill disrespectful commoners on the spot.

Samurai skills consisted of swordsmanship, archery, horsemanship and the use of the spear. There was also a tradition of "bunbu ryodo", which means the pen and the sword, both ways. Samurai were not only expected to be proficient at fighting skills but they were also expected to be educated and cultured. During the peaceful Tokugawa period, some samurai easily evolved into management roles. Other ronin (masterless samurai) became farmers or merchants. Women of the samurai class would also often have knowledge and expertise in certain weapons, in particular the naginata, a spear with a curved blade. The same code applied to samurai women although of course they had different responsibilities. Honour and duty were paramount.

Many stories are told to illustrate the virtues of the samurai. One of the most popular stories "The 47 Ronin" was made into a Kabuki play, Kanadehon Chushingura. In 1702, Lord Enya Hangan was forced to commit ritual suicide when he drew his sword and wounded a rival in the shogun's palace. His loyal samurai believed that he had been forced into this transgression and vowed to avenge his death. Although it took years of patience, planning and self sacrifice, their goal was eventually achieved.

The selfless existence demanded by the bushido code was aided and enriched by the concept of Zen, which was introduced at about the same time in the twelfth century AD. Zen is more of a philosophy than a religion but it was wholeheartedly embraced by the samurai class. Zen like other forms of Buddhism teaches that individualism and the physical world around us is an illusion. Enlightenment will come through freedom from illusion and passion. The intellect deceives us, intuition and spontaneity are to be prized as they come from the true self. We are one with the world.

Zen Buddhism is however a very positive type of Buddhism, advocating action rather than words, self discipline through physical hardships, self cultivation for a higher purpose and dedication to the Way, i.e. in this case the way of the sword.

The philosophy of "ai-uchi", mutual striking down, results from training in Zen. One of the greatest swordsmen of the Kashima Shintoryu was a teacher of Budo, called Bokuden Tsukara. Records show that he killed his first opponent at the age of seventeen and subsequently fought in many battles, escaping with only

Uyeshiba Morihei, founder of Aikido.

wounds from arrows. He also fought nineteen duels with a live blade.

One such battle was against an expert with sword and naginata called Kajiwara Nagato. Nagato was so good that he could cut down birds in flight. Nevertheless his followers were worried about the impending match and they urged him to reconsider the challenge. Nagato replied "There are always strong and weak things. It is due to an opponent's unskilled technique that I am able to cut both his arms with my spear. It is not so easy to defeat a skilled man armed with a long sword but my naginata is the same as a short bladed spear, even if I am cut I will not die without defeating him".

Such a philosophical attitude was attained through the practise of Zen. Self control and self discipline enabled him to believe that his own death was not the real issue. He could therefore do what he had to do without fear. A famous master in the Edo period wrote a poem containing the following extract: "Forge the spirit according to the divine will; seek the heat and light of the universal sword and move on toward enlightenment." This was his reality.

Even through the peaceful times of the Tokugawa period, when samurai no longer required for battle often became masterless ronin, the bushido code was held out as one of the highest laws in the land. Only during the Meiji period, when the samurai were disestablished and a conscript army of all classes was raised, were the principles and ideals of the samurai overcome by western influence. The samurai were driven into revolt against the Government through the commutation of pensions and the anti-sword laws. A samurai's sword was his soul. Until the anti-sword laws he could wear two swords. In spirit, the rebels were true to the emperor and to their code. They believed that the Government was being false and faithless, not themselves. The rebellion of samurai at Satsuma lead by Takamori Saigo resulted in a victory for the conscript army and seemed to mark the end of samurai supremacy and Bushido.

Yet, could a code of ethics which had been so widely held for so many centuries then cease to exist? In "Bushido the Soul of Japan", Inazo Nitobe states that "Bushido as an independent code of ethics may vanish, but its power will not perish from the earth". "The Spirit of Budo" by Trevor Leggett illustrates the value of these traditional virtues in the present day life. Bushido, now Budo, is part and parcel of modem Japanese martial arts and there is no way that you can study Aikido without regard to it.

The great changes which the Emperor Meiji introduced to bring Japan out of its isolation, affected certain men who would have great influence in the world of martial arts. Dr Jigoro Kano (1860-1936) travelled throughout Japan studying jujitsu from various Masters. He gradually developed Judo, meaning the gentle way. In 1882 he founded the world headquarters of Judo, the Kodokan in Tokyo and started to train his first disciples in this art. By eliminating the most dangerous moves, those which would kill or maim, he brought jujitsu into the new Japan as Judo.

Morihei Ueshiba (1883-1969) was already very knowledgeable in the martial arts when he met Sokaku Takeda and decided to study at the Daitokan at Hokkaido. Takeda had travelled Japan teaching his family system before finally settling here and opening the Daitokan. His ancestor was Shinra Saburo Yoshimitsu, of the Minamoto clan, the famous general who developed Daito-ryu Aiki-jujitsu.

Ueshiba became involved with the Omoto religion (a Shinto sect), through the influence of the Onisaburo Deguchi in 1919. He accompanied Deguchi to Manchuria and Mongolia in 1924, where they hoped to set up a utopian colony. When this venture failed, He returned to Tokyo and taught Daito ryu Aiki-jujitsu at various places until he established the Kobukan dojo in 1931. He gradually distanced himself from Takeda and after about eleven years started to call his art Aiki Budo.

Shortly after the outbreak of the Second World War, he gave up his teaching posts in Tokyo, which included several military schools.*e retired to Iwama, where he devoted himself to training, meditation and farming. This is where Aikido was further developed. During the mid-1950's, he spent a lot of time teaching in Tokyo. He travelled to a certain extent but less and less as his health became frail. He died of liver cancer on 26th April 1969.

Ueshiba's principles included the policy of complete non aggression. An attack would be neutralised by the coordination of movement, a lead or a bypass to control the attacker with the very minimum force. He taught tens of thousands of students during a fifty year teaching career.

Many of his pupils were sent abroad to teach the new art. Koichi Tohei went to Hawaii, where he taught the police. He also spent seven years in the USA and taught special units of the American armed forces. On his return to Japan he became the chief instructor at the Aikikai Hombu, the headquarters of Aikido set up by Ueshiba in Tokyo. Following a disagreement with Ueshiba's son Kisshomaru and other teachers, he left to found the Shinshin Toitsu Aikidokai, where he could emphasise the development of ki through exercises.

Yoshimitsu Yamada was another pupil sent to teach in the USA. He is head of the New York Aikikai. Tadashi Abe studied law at the Sorbonne in France and did much to promote Aikido in France. Gozo Shioda, the director of the Aikido

Yoshinkan was the head instructor to the Tokyo Metropolitan Police force. His pupils have done much to promote the Yoshinkan system throughout the world.

Kenji Tomiki studied Judo under Dr Kano and went on to learn Aikido under Ueshiba in 1926. He patterned his Aikido after the ideas of Jigoro Kano's Judo and
developed it as a competitive sport. Many of Tomiki's students travelled and taught abroad. Senta Yamada, who was also taught by Ueshiba arrived in Great Britain and soon established Tomiki Aikido there. Takeshi Inoue also taught in England for three years.

As Ueshiba's pupils developed their own styles and spread them throughout the world, so their own disciples have started their own Aikido clubs, federations and societies. The addresses of clubs in the Aikido Union may be obtained from Pat Stratford – see Acknowledgements. A further list of clubs and Aikidoka may be found in "The Aiki News Encyclopedia of Aikido" by Stanley A. Pranin.

When practising Aikido you should not "look with blinkers', i.e. you should be aware of different ways. When you practise in a club you should keep the same open mind. See if the principles of Aikido are being followed. See if the ethics of Budo are honoured. Loyalty and faith in an instructor are not blind or one way. He also has obligations and a duty to you.

Miyamoto Musashi, the famous swordsman of the 16th century stated "The teacher is as a needle, the disciple is as the thread. You must practise constantly." His Book of the Five Rings (Go Rin No Sho), is a classic guide to both swordsmanship and strategy, used by martial artists and modem businessmen alike. Things could not have been so different when he wrote it as he says "If we look at the world we see arts for sale. Men use equipment to sell their own selves. As if with the nut and the flower, the nut has become less than the flower. In this kind of Way of strategy, both those teaching and those learning the way are as concerned with colouring and showing off their technique, trying to hasten the bloom of the flower. They are looking for profit. Someone once said 'immature strategy is the cause of grief'. That was a true saying."

In Japan, admittance to a Dojo is usually by reference or recommendation. not everyone is accepted. Children are sent by parents to develop their bodies, mind and spirit. Training often includes periods of meditation and spiritual guidance. They are not sent just for self defence as in this country. The long tradition of courtesy and self discipline in Japan means that violence is very rare. Women and children are safe to walk about even at night. This is slowly changing through the western influence. Would that we could change our world for the better through Aikido.

In Budo of all types, those practising begin and end with a salutation. In Aikido we start and finish with a rei, also to our partners. The Aikidoka gives his partner respect and exercises prudence in his training. Through this practise, he develops and leads himself from the stage of self discipline to the capacity for self defence and there after to higher spiritual levels.

For these reasons good manners, etiquette and the correct attitude to training are also important. Do not be concerned with "winning". We have a saying "to win is to lose and to lose is to win". If you are in a hurry to succeed you will not become skilful. Skill will come with a little guidance and a lot of practise, a little thinking, a lot of action, a little talking and a lot of doing.

The correct attitude is to leave all problems, bitterness, anger behind when you step on the tatami. Be prepared to train with and learn by training with anyone. Help others and receive their cooperation in return. Goodwill is passed onwards as is illwill. When you help someone less experienced, you will often find that certain factors become clearer or other factors fall into place.

Don't fritter your energy away talking. Try to keep a clear mind when practising. Always complete your movement. You will never know if a technique is possible until the movement has been finished. If it does not work, think "what didn't I do?" Fill in the missing factors. It's no good thinking "what did I do wrong?" The answer could be "everything!"

Observe and try to emulate what has been shown by your instructor. Watch his posture, his feet movements, his hand and arm movements, the movement of his centre. Obviously you cannot take all this in at once, so watch for different things each time it is shown. Watch also the posture of the attacker; when he is taken off posture and how he is controlled. 75% of all movement is hidden. 25% you will not understand. Begin to understand the 25%, then you will see the hidden 75%.

Chapter 1

FIRST STEPS

In the beginning there is chaos: two left feet and flailing arms. Starting Aikido is like learning to walk all over again. Once on the mat (tatami), you realise that you can't stand up straight let alone walk. One touch and you fall down.

Good posture is essential in Aikido, whether you are moving or stationary. This doesn't mean that you stand stiffly to attention like a soldier on parade, but relaxed, particularly at the joints, with a straight back and looking ahead not down.

Some schools insist that you take a particular stance. This is not necessary or desirable. It limits your flexibility and movement, slowing down your movement. This may mean moving one leg forward or backwards and or to either side.

However, when you move your legs, the problem is that you must also move your centre. The centre by tradition is the point just below the navel. Now this may confuse you. How to move your legs with your centre? Your centre is the storehouse of all your power and energy (ki). All movement starts and coordinates with your centre. So you ask how to move your legs with your centre? The answer is only with practice.

The exercises that we do before a training session will help especially "tai sabaki". I will not describe tai sabaki as you will learn it in training and as explained earlier this guide is meant to supplement training not replace it.

When you do tai sabaki try to move your hips first then let your legs finish the movement. When you have turned in your tai sabaki to face the opposite direction, your hips should have turned to the extent that you immediately unwind as you tai sabaki back. In this way you will train yourself to move centre

Figure 1: Attack shomen, with correct maai, Uke must take a step to reach you.

Figures 2, 3: Absorb, deflect so Uke (1) is drawn into your sphere.

first and your movement will be continuous.

If you take big steps you'll find it very difficult to do this. In fact you'll probably find it difficult to move at all at this stage of your training. Tai sabaki is a circular movement. When you move keep your weight evenly distributed, i.e. directed down from your centre. If your weight is on one foot you can only move the other one. This limits your flexibility and movement. This may not seem important when your instructor has specified an attack and the technique but later on when you have learnt the techniques, your movements should be automatic and spontaneous so that you can cope with any attack.

The freedom of movement is vital in Aikido. You must learn to move in any direction and your movements must flow and be continuous. I sometimes explain that its like pushing a heavy wheel barrow up a hill. If you keep pushing it will keep going and when you get to the top it will race down the other side. However if you stop you have an awful job to get going again. Sometimes it's impossible especially for a beginner.

The proper distance between you and your opponent is called Maai. This is when you are safe out of reach. Stretch out your arms and turn a complete circle. This is your sphere. In this sphere you may remain on posture and be strong. But this also applies to your opponent so enter his sphere and you may be overpowered. When your opponent takes a step forward to attack you, he enters your sphere and if you can harmonise your movements with his you can take him off posture. Here you would need to absorb, lead, deflect and project. Your other alternative is to enter his sphere at a strategic moment so that you and your sphere, dominate and take him off posture.

Whatever movement or technique you do, you must be on posture and your opponent must be taken off posture otherwise it is a battle of strength not skill. Obviously in a battle of strength the biggest and strongest will win. Using skill, the small and weak often have an advantage; if they know they can't use strength, they don't try.

Coming back to the situation where your opponent attacks you and enters your sphere, if you move back slightly, i.e. move your left leg back so that you are in a stance, he will have overreached slightly. This is enough for him to be off posture. You have absorbed. Now any numbers of options will be open to you.

You can practice this without touching each other (or taking hold). You must harmonise your movements with his and not vice versa. If he takes, you must lead or absorb. Again this is nothing that you can learn from a book. You must train and practice. Leading exercises are a must. A lead is not a pull. A lead always

Figure 4: Enter his sphere at a strategic moment.

25

comes to or bypasses your centre.

If you decide to enter the attacker's sphere instead of absorbing or leading, your timing is crucial. You must be in before the attack is unstoppable. Only practice will teach you this awareness (zanshin). Try to see the whole picture in front of you not just his hand or his arm. Certainly don't look into his eyes, you will be drawn into them. Move in without thinking. Thoughts slow you down or even stop you moving in the first place. Remember how hard it was to get out of bed this morning? Anyway move in without thinking. Once he is off posture, again all the techniques are available to you.

A famous Japanese swordsman once said, "My enemy stands before me, I draw my sword and I am in Hell. I take one step forward and I am in Heaven." Thinking about something gives us a problem and we torment ourselves with the finding the solution. Once we act here is no problem to pore over.

It should now be very clear to you that the first thing that you do is the most important. If you do not have your opponent off posture you cannot control him. If you cannot control him, you cannot do technique (except by lucky fluke). You will also find that if you are not in control, then he probably is!

The closer you work to your centre, the more power you will have. You cannot work on the edge of your sphere. This is why you absorb an opponent into your sphere so that you have more power and control. Once you have control, keep it and keep good posture. Make your opponent move, rather than moving yourself and leaving him upright. Controlling factors are many and varied and must be learnt.

One way of controlling is by "taking the slack". This means that when someone has hold of you, you do not move their arm about and leave the body upright. To have any effect on their body or centre, you must ensure that their arm is taut. You might do this by stretching it out but more effectively by turning it by turning your own wrist. Sankyo and Kote gaeshi are good examples of this. Another control is by use of the hand on the neck or shoulder to stop him from turning away, i.e. in iriminage.

As I said before, the very first thing that you do is the most important. If you can't start a technique you certainly can't finish it. I had a teacher once who fooled all of us for a while by instructing us "just to go for a walk". The technique was then supposed to magically fall into place. Of course it did for him but not for us! It is not a matter of walking, nothing could be further from the truth. Most people walk just with their legs: see them bob up and down. Now watch the Masters

Figure 5: With an attack from yokomen…

Figure 6: the left hip moves in to pin and control…

Figure 7: and the right hip moves through as Tori (r) throws.

sway from side to side. They use their hips.

Your centre or your hips always move first. Our eyes often deceive us in Aikido. It may look as if that arm or hand waves about first but I assure you that it must be coordinated with the centre to have the desired effect. As for the walk, when you move it is vital to move correctly.

As a general guide, the hip closest to your opponent will help you to do the throwing or controlling. The other hip or side of the body should be used to get you in the right place or to get your opponent off posture (We commonly say to pin or obtain a pin).

In a throwing technique, you should be moving the hip closest to your opponent past his centre as you execute the throw, e.g. tenchi nage. In a controlling technique, your centres should be compatible. In practice this means that your hip is level with his or opposite as in ikkyo. You hips should be close. Your hips rise and fall naturally as you turn.

Your first move will usually be an oblique one rather than straight backwards, forwards or sideways. This is how you will be able to deflect the attack and take your opponent off posture.

I had a class full of kids one time walking around like robots; right arm, right leg together, left arm left leg together. We had some fun but it made them realise how to coordinate their bodies.

There is no other comparison between a mechanical movement and Aikido. Once you have learned where to put your feet and move your hips, you must not stop at each stage. It must all flow into one movement.

Aikido should start as a gentle breeze and finish like a tomado. You should build up momentum and power by your movements. If your movements are circular they can go on to infinity. If you use straight lines you must have to stop to change direction.

Without using your centre, your arms or legs rely solely upon their muscle and strength. If you move your centre or hips and your arms or legs move with them, then they rely on the power of your centre. Imagine that you have a bolt between your right arm and right hip. As you move your hip forward, your arm moves with the power of your centre. You should say that the ki is flowing from your centre through your arm. This is the beginnings of the power of movement.

Again if your arms move independently you will try to use muscles and strength, which your opponent feels as aggression. He reacts to this. You must try never to give aggression for this reason. If you do not use strength but the power from your centre (ki), there is no aggression and nothing to fight.

Exercises, particularly leading exercises improve coordination, harmony and ki.

Ki is the Spirit in Aikido, Ai being the harmony. Ki is not some magical, mysterious force Star Wars style, but an energy which builds within you. On one level Ki is the undefatigable spirit which will not bow down, which continues until what was intended has been done no matter what the obstacles. On another level it is the use of the centre which I have already mentioned. By coordination ki flows from the centre through the arms, through out the legs. It can be directed or redirected through certain points like the chin, the elbows, the fingers.

Instructors often used to show the unbendable arm as an example of ki. Energy flowed through the arm, relaxed, curved but stretched out. The arm could not be bent. One Japanese instructor demanded to be shown this unbendable arm. He redirected the ki by a kote gaeshi and turning movement, saying "Yes very good ki, I piss on your Ki!"

You will find that if you move into an attackers sphere (an entering technique is called irimi), even if you coordinate your unbendable arm and centre, if you allow your arm to bend your power will evaporate and your technique will collapse with it.

It is interesting that you can use an opponent's ki against him and the reverse is also true that he can use your ki against you.

For example in kote gaeshi if the elbow points down and you continue the motion downwards, he goes down. If we point it out and again you continue your motion in that direction he is sent flying. In tenchi nage, beginners commonly weigh down on another's shoulders. They are pouring their ki into their attacker and giving them power to resist. Their ki should flow over the opponent and down their back into the tatami, where the opponent will then land.

Take irimi nage from ushiro, a common mistake is to jab the opponent with the elbow and to expect him to fall. In fact he reacts to the aggression but finds it easy to direct the ki along the line of your arm from the elbow towards the fingers. The answer is to redirect the ki before he has chance to stop you. If the arm is continuing in a circular movement then ki is flowing until your movement is

Figure 8: Uke takes in ushiro ryote tori and controls Tori's ki.

Figure 9: Tori re-directs ki in a circular movement.

Figure 10: Uke falls.

over. In all techniques the opponent should be falling before you have finished your movement.

Ki will flow if you are relaxed but controlled. Relaxed and floppy is one extreme, tense and tight is the other. If you train often your movements will become automatic rather than thought controlled. Then they will become relaxed. Try too hard and you will be come tense.

A Zen story tells us that there once was woodcutter who went out into the forest every day to cut down trees. One day he became aware of a creature who hid every time he looked at him. The creature laughed at him and said that he would never be able to catch him because he could read the woodcutters mind. He became so annoyed with this creature that he determined to kill it. Yet every time that he turned around the creature was gone. He took many a hopeless swipe with his axe before he decided that he was wasting his time. He gave up trying to kill the creature and turned back to his tree felling. Suddenly the head flew loose from the axe handle and accidentally hit the creature, killing him in one fell swoop.

Keep training and practising without trying to hit your target. The results will also surprise you.

Make a fist and you put a stopper on your ki. Stretch out your fingers and imagine that it is flowing to infinity way past your opponent. Again there are exercises to perform to make mind and body aware of ki. I will mention them later. Exercises are as important for the mind as for the body. Many of us in the western world make no attempt at all to control our minds. But it must be controlled to prevent aggression, domination of the ego, frustration, jealousy and all the other attitudes which interfere with training and with the rest of our lives.

When an opponent is attacking you, you can change the course of his ki by deflecting the blow or attack. A deflection is not a block. If someone hits you on your head and you don't move, the force of the blow makes you go down. If you put your arm over your head to block it, the force of the blow continues through your arm, head and body downwards just the same, (unless you have a bionic arm). Blocks are never used in Aikido because you still have to take the force of the blow. A deflection alters the course of the blow so that you do not take the full

The direction in which you face is important because this also affects the way you turn your centre and the direction of your ki. You will realise this later on. A kiai, a shout coming from your centre gives you extra power at the moment of contact. The sound and vibrations can also unnerve your attacker.

Chapter 2

BASIC EXERCISES

An exercise is a movement which becomes automatic through repeated actions. If it is automatic then there is no need to think about what you are doing. The result is that your action is over before you have thought about it or before your opponent has time to think about it or stop it.

Ever been driving along thinking about the meeting you're on your way to or the shopping that you're going to buy? You don't have to concentrate on the mechanics of driving. In the context of Aikido, which is an Art designed for multiple attacks, you will eventually be able to direct your mind to the attackers further along the road, rather than the one who currently faces you. Dealing with him will be as effortless as driving that car.

But first we have to build the automatic responses. Practice the mechanics on your own by all means but you will only know if you are doing it correctly when you are on the tatami with an opponent or partner and the exercise has the desired effect.

The exercises which follow will build the correct responses for basic attacks and more. I do not include exercises for fitness and flexibility as these are self evident and need no explanation.

Study not just the actions but the effect on your partner, (uke). Repeat the exercises on both sides. The photographs show simply the movements. Try to imagine the flow of your ki. This is what you should be emulating by your lead or movement.

Exercise 1
Imagine a circle in the vertical plane which defines the outskirts of your power. Bring your hands from your centre straight up above your head then stretch them out to the sides and back to your centre again. Turn your hands into praying position as they rise and turn them palm outwards as they stretch out, palms back together as they return to centre.

Figure 11: Stand in a natural posture.

Figure 12: Describe a circle with your arms.

Reverse this exercise after a few times. Imagine gathering in energy from the world. This exercise will help you, for example when you sweep away a punch (tsuki) and go into tenchi nage.

Exercise 2

Stand, heels together, hands relaxed at your sides but level with your centre. Move your centre forward and down by gliding one leg forward, knee slightly bent, foot turned outwards. As you move bring your hands in a curved movement level with your face. Your hands should be relaxed so that your fingers are curved. Turn your hands as you lift them so that from being palms up at your centre they are now palms facing down when raised. Feel the power moving from your centre. Move back, then forwards again without hesitation. This exercise will help you to enter positively, (all irimi techniques).

Exercise 3

Stand as in exercise 2, and move forward in the same way. As you move forwards, move your hands forwards, palms upmost. As they reach their limit turn them downwards and point back towards your centre. At this time your centre should be moving back. Your hands should be moving back with your centre. Imagine waves washing on a shore. This is your motion. Again try to feel the power of your movement. As soon as you have moved back, you should be moving forwards again. Kokyu nage is a good example of techniques where this exercise is useful.

Exercise 4

Stand in posture. You are going to tai sabaki. With right leg forward, stretch out your left hand. As you start to turn, direct your fingers to your centre. They reach your centre in the middle of your turn and stretch out again when you have completed your movement. Change legs. Feel the power in your arms coming from the centre. Keep the fingers and wrist flexible so that they continually twist and turn in the right direction. This exercise is good for leading into any technique. Never stretch too far from your centre. Keep fingers relaxed and curved.

13

14

Figures 13, 14: Move your centre by gliding forwards; hands do not stretch out of your sphere.

Figures 15, 16, 17: As you reach your limit, point to your centre, drawing back your hands and centering.

15

16

17

18

19

Figure 18: Stand in posture, right leg forwards, left hand ready to lead to your centre as you turn.

Figure 19: Finish your tai sabaki with both hands in front of your centre.

Exercise 5

Stand in posture. Turn on the balls of your feet to face the opposite direction. Keep your posture and coordinate the movement of your hands. (Right hand moves with right hip, left hand with left hip.)

Exercise 6

You are taken in gyaku katate tori (right hand takes right hand or vice versa). Wind your wrist inwards as you turn your hip (right hand, right hip and vice versa), ready to step obliquely outwards. Keep elbows down and move arm and leg together as you step out. Your opponent (uke), should be turned away from you and off posture. You should be on posture.

The effect of winding your wrist is to tighten up the tendons in his arm and give you control over is body so that when you move he also must move. This is often referred to as taking the slack up. If there is slack in his arm, you will only move the arm not the body.

He should also feel that this is a natural movement for him. Don't try to make his arm go where it is unable to go or push him away. If you move with your centre and coordinate movements correctly his arm will have moved in a nice upward curve as his body turns away from you.

Since now he is off posture and in no position to attack you, various options are open to you. Shihonage is perhaps the most obvious.

Exercise 7

Again from gyaku kakate tori, turn your wrist inwards so that it is nearly palm down as you take uke's wrist with your other hand. At the same time absorb the attack by drawing back the relevant hip (same arm, same hip) and leading the hand towards it. Release your wrist from his grip as you tai sabaki and lead him around you. You will finish your movement facing the opposite direction. Finish the circular movement of your lead by curling your hand back to your centre.

Uke should be off posture as soon as you turn your wrist. He should be off posture as you lead him around you. You are the centre of the circle and he must travel all the way around you. Don't make jerky movements or bend your arm at the elbow. Don't drag him from behind you. Your lead is a forward motion

Figure 20: From a stance, turn on the balls
of your feet.

Figure 21: Coordinate hands with your
turning movement.

Figure 22: Uke takes in gyaku
katate tori.

Figure 23: Turn the wrist anti-clockwise
without lifting to deflect the attack.

Figure 24: Enter obliquely.

Figure 25: Absorb the attack and take his wrist.

Figure 26: Lead Uke around you.

Figure 27: Finish at your centre.

Figure 28: Coordinate hip and wrist movement (clockwise).

Figure 29: Enter to take Uke's centre.

Figure 30: Turn your wrist and direct to your centre.

Figure 31: As Uke gathers momentum towards you, move forwards.

Figure 32: Deflect by moving obliquely to the left.

powered by the movement of your centre. The larger the radius of the circle in which you lead him, the further he will have to travel, the more he will be off posture.

Exercise 8

This is an entering movement. As uke takes your wrist in gyaku katate tori, turn it outwards and move (same leg, same arm) into his sphere. Although the wrist has turned, the arm goes straight towards him as your centre moves forward to take his centre. The turning of the wrist will start to take up any slack and your entering movement should take him off posture so that he is leaning backwards over his centre.

If you have this position correct you will be able to continue your motion forwards and downwards to his centre to execute a throw. Do not bend your arm at the elbow too much. Just keep a slight curve of the arm. Don't push. As in all Aikido you must take him off posture, before you are able to execute your throw.

The movement of your whole arm is circular because as you are moving in, it is also curving downwards like a cut.

Exercise 9

From gyaku kakate tori, wind your wrist inwards and direct to your centre as you move backwards. Keep looking in the same direction. As you move backwards your wrist sweeps past your centre and behind you. The effect of this is to draw uke downwards and towards you. Then as he gathers speed he is directed past you as you move past him.

You must not bend your arm at the elbow. You must not pull. The movement is a downwards curve towards the centre and past it. Uke is moving forwards, off posture, under your control so this would be a good beginning for any irimi technique.

Exercise 10

Uke takes your right hand with his right hand. Step out obliquely with your left leg then back into him with your right leg coordinating your movement so that your right wrist and forearm turn into him also. This is similar to exercise 8 but now you have started to tai sabaki. Continue this movement and as you do, lead uke so that he spirals down around you. Do not reach. Finish the lead at your centre.

Figure 33: Enter, taking Uke's centre.

Figures 34, 35: Lead him so that he spirals down around you.

Figure 36: Uke takes in ryote tori.

Figure 37: Coordinate your movement to take his centre.

Exercise 11

You are taken by both hands (ryote tori). Wind one wrist outwards and downwards to your centre at the same time as you turn the relative hip back. The other wrist moves forward with the other hip and winds inwards. Imagine if one hip moves forward the other must be back in relation to it. If the arms move with the hips then they also must go one forward, one slightly back. The arm that goes back goes down, the one that goes forward goes up to take the uke's centre.

Movement there must be synchronised. As one arm moves in one direction so the other moves in the opposite. When held in a grip like two iron bars, you must bend the pillars of strength outwards. It is important to turn these wrists more so that the iron bars are bent and the power in them is reduced. Obviously strength will not work, the arms are only extensions of the centre.

Remember this exercise when you perform tenchi nage, or later sumiotoshi or tsuke.

Chapter 3

BASIC TECHNIQUES

Just because something is called a basic technique doesn't mean that it is going to be easy. Quite the contrary. It is basic because it is a basic building block without which you cannot progress. Techniques are nothing more than learning exercises which teach you the principles of Aikido and educate you in movement, coordination, synchronisation of movement, maai, posture and spirit.

A beginner will start out with no knowledge of movement or technique and he will be surprisingly successful because he doesn't know what he is doing. He just has faith in the teacher. As he learns more he will start to puzzle more and needs to understand what he is doing. Thought processes whilst practising, will spoil techniques. He will start to realise how difficult it is. He will start to feel that he is getting worse not better.

For a Master there are no techniques because his movements together with all the other qualities and skills that he has developed are sufficient to ensure that he moves in the correct way and is in the right place at the right time, doing the right thing. In a way he is like that beginner, except that he has faith in himself rather than the instructor.

In this chapter, I am not going to describe each technique, step by step. You must be taught the basics on the tatami and see how the movements flow. Each throw or technique must be one movement not 1-2-3. What I will be doing is showing how each technique may relate to a basic exercise (there are many other beginnings for each technique) and how the principles apply in this case.

By basic I mean from an attack of gyaku katate tori (right hand takes right hand or vice versa). As a rule only allow someone to take hold if you want them to and then you must control straight away. Otherwise you move as soon as they start to move so that you absorb or deflect. If you stand where you are you could be held static by an attacker on posture in their own sphere and you will be helpless.

Figure 38: Deflect by stepping obliquely.

Figure 39: Enter coordinating the arms and lifting.

Figure 40: Uke is falling as you turn.

Figure 41: Maintain good posture as he falls.

1   Shihonage

This a four ways throw. In Japan four like eight is also used as a meaning for many. So you are moving in many directions.

For shihonage (irimi), your first movement is to turn your wrist and sweep their arm away from you (as per exercise 6). This is a deflection of the attack. Hip and arm move together obliquely, then move your other hip then leg close and past his centre. Lift the arm as you move in. Your other arm should be making contact with his arm to assist in this as you move.

Your movement makes uke turn away from you and takes him off posture. Turn and bring his arm downwards AS you turn NOT after you turn.

The direction is a circular arch downwards. Do not take the arm outwards, you could damage it. This is an advanced throw not for beginners. If you lift your arm too high to go under it, uke will twirl and avoid the throw because you have let out the slack and lost control. So don't take it too high, keep it controlled with the hand in front of your face as you turn.

Shihonage (tenkan) is a bypass of his power. Turn your wrist again and holding his wrist with both hands, tai sabaki around until you are behind him. Take big steps and stay as relaxed as possible. Again you should be taking him down as you are moving not after you finished your move. Move from your centre not shoulders or you will be stopped.

2   Kote gaeshi

This is a controlling throw or take down. Contrary to commonly held belief this does not mean twisting the wrist until pain forces uke to submit or until lasting damage is done. When properly applied the slack in the arm is taken up to the extent that when the arm is moved, the body is also controlled. You will see a bend in one's elbow when this occurs.

Start this technique by taking uke's wrist with your other hand and turning outwards by tai sabaki (exercise 7). As you turn lead the wrist downwards towards your centre. This is a circular movement in a horizontal plane. Add the other hand to support the wrist and keep it controlled and alter the circle to a vertical one leading down into the tatami or straight down your centre into the tatami.

Figure 42: Kote gaeshi is a control. Note elbow bend.

Figure 43: Take Uke in kote gaeshi as you absorb, leading him around you.

Figure 44: Uke falls as you make a circle either in the vertical plane or by leading him down.

Figure 45: Keep hold if you wish to control.

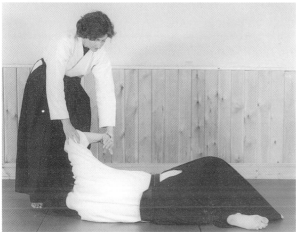

Figure 46: Turn Uke face down.

47

Figure 47: A suitable immobilisation.

Keep control of the wrist throughout by use of the three smallest fingers, especially the little finger, keep movements continuous and flowing. Do not pull the wrist from behind you, but lead from your centre.

If uke took hold of your wrist before you started the movement, you would have to turn your own wrist so that your hand can escape, but before you do so take loosely with your other hand so that you maintain control.

3   Tenchi nage

This is heaven and earth throw. Your ki flows up to heaven, over uke's shoulder and back to earth on the other side of him. Too many beginners rest on uke's shoulder and give away all their power or swing their arm across him horizontally only to be stopped because uke saw it coming.

Sweep away the attack using your hand and hip obliquely (i.e. left arm, left hip deflects his right hand). This should take him off posture as in exercise 11, but don't stop your movement. Bring your other hand upwards from your centre so that it can't be seen. Keep the hand turned palm towards yourself. As the arm goes over the shoulder, turn your hand so that it faces uke's back. As it goes over, your hip should be turning and moving through behind him.

If the leg goes through without turning the hip, you will be off posture and vulnerable. The hip on the outside moves you into position and gives the pin, i.e. takes him off posture. The hip closest to uke turns to throw him.

4   Ikkyo

Ikkyo is arm pin. Some people hold the elbow down on the tatami, but this should really be a control, based on tendons or nerves from shoulder to arm. Stretch his arm out on the tatami, elbow uppermost at say one o'clock. With your free hand scoop from shoulder to the elbow and stop at a point just above the elbow. Your knees should be tight against the arm, one in the arm pit, one at the wrist. On your knees keep your body high until you have everything in position. Then sink your centre downwards, applying pressure. Toes should not be flat but turned ready for you to get up quickly if necessary.

You may start ikkyo by way of exercise 8. Bring up the other leg/hip close and with a turning motion of your own body, lead uke's arm to your centre. Your free

Figure 48: Deflect Uke's attack and enter obliquely.

Figure 49: Left arm goes up to 'heaven' and down to 'earth' as the hip goes through.

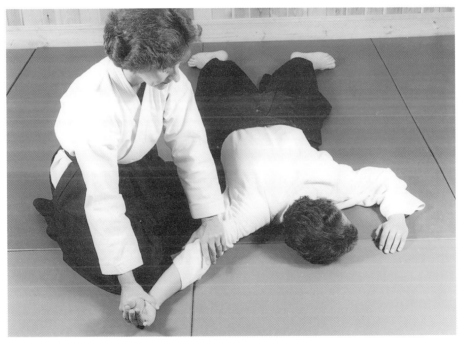

Figure 50: Ikkyo is an arm pin.

Figure 51: Enter deeply as in exercise 8.

Figure 52: Lead his arm to your centre as you move through.

Figure 53: Lead Uke around you

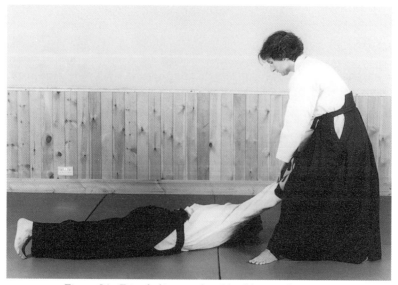

Figure 54: Tai sabaki around and lead him to the tatami.

arm should be making contact with his side as soon as you move in, your hand taking hold above the elbow. Both arms work together with your centre.

As he starts to go downwards, move the turning hip through so that your leg makes contact with his body. This gives you more control. Take uke down into the tatami by moving yourself and the arm out at an angle and leading to your centre.

For ikkyo you obviously want uke to take hold of your wrist. For a tenkan movement, enter and start his turning motion by use of your arms and hips. This time do not step into the V made by his body and arm but turn outwards and spin him around with you. Keep the movement spiralling downwards. Keep contact, if you wish to take down. This can also be a throw.

Although in the west shihonage and techi nage are often the first techniques to be taught, it is interesting to note that in Japan the order would be:

(1) Ikkyo
(2) Nikkyo
(3) Sankkyo
(4) Yonkkyo
(5) Gokkyo

The first five numbers in Japanese are: ichi, ni, san, shi or yon, and go. The above techniques therefore mean first, second, third, fourth and fifth lessons of technique. However, I will continue with my own numbering.

5   Nikkyo

Nikkyo is another one of those controls that to most people simply means pain. It always seems strange that the least effort you put into a technique, the better it works. Nikkyo is a case in point. It is difficult for a beginner to understand the amount of discomfort he is inflicting. As with all techniques, release uke as soon as he taps.

To make this simple, you can start from exercise 8. Turn slightly to the side and wind your hand over his wrist, using those three fingers again. Little finger first, wind one, two, three into your own centre. From the beginning your free hand should be resting on his in a clingy way so that he doe not escape yet neither does he feel any aggression.

As he is going down you can move your centre forwards so that he falls backwards or you can take his elbow and with a turning movement lead him down into the tatami.

Figure 55: Nikkyo – note the bend in the elbow.

Figure 56: Turn to the side and wind your hand over his wrist.

Figure 57: Direct your fingers to your own centre.

Figure 58: An immobilisation for Nikkyo.

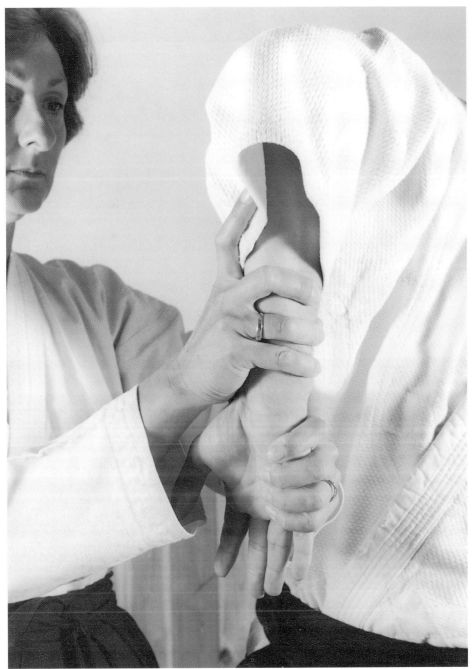

Figure 59: Yonkkyo.

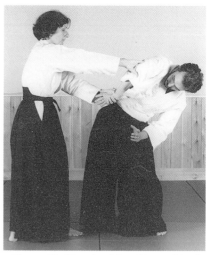

Figure 60: Enter and take the hand as you tai sabaki.

Figure 61: Finish your movement safely behind Uke.

Figure 62: Turn back into him and lead down.

Figure 63: Maintain the Sankkyo throughout.

Figure 64: An immobilisation.

6 Sankkyo

This may again be started from exercise 8. Tai sabaka around and take uke's hand with three fingers – little finger first. Unravel uke's hand by rolling down the hand which he took if necessary. Take sankkyo as you move and finish a little behind him. When you have a hold, turn your body back towards uke. This will tighten the control, but only if you move with your centre rather than your arms.

The angle which his arm makes should be 90 degrees. His hand and forearm should make a straight line downwards. Don't bend the hand in. Don't try to twist the wrist off. You could cause lasting damage and still not have control. Pain controls some people but not all.

If you have a sankkyo and you move same arm, same hip backwards, uke will move with you. If you hold the sankkyo from a little behind him, your arm making contact with his body, he will be unable to turn and hit you because he will be causing himself pain.

You can throw forwards using same arm, same hip and downwards in a circular movement. You can throw backwards by continuing your turning movement into uke and downwards. This will not be successful if you use your arm and strength rather than your centre and movement. You can also take down into the tatami if you keep turning into him until you are facing and he is off posture. Without waiting smooth one hand up his arm to the elbow and in a scooping movement him downwards to the tatami via your centre.

Another way is to make a V between your thumb and other fingers. Take his wrist in this V and move arm and centre obliquely away from him so that his arm starts to form an arch. Move deeply under this arch and keep turning. The sankkyo comes on automatically.

Do not squeeze the wrist tightly. Try to keep a firm, fixed hold with the wrist supported by the thumb. Sometimes the other hand is also used on the arm to increase the control. This is like a sword hold. If someone has such a large hand that you feel that sankkyo is impossible, take the fingers only.

7 Yonkyo

Start with exercise 8 and move as for sankkyo. The wrist that uke has taken turns in his grip so that our hand can take hold of his. When you place your other hand and you will see that your hands are now the opposite way to sankkyo. Correctly performed you will catch a nerve in uke's wrist.

You now have a grip like a sword and you can lead into the tatami with a movement like a sword cut.

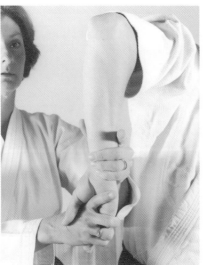

Figure 65: Enter and turn as for sankkyo.

Figures 66, 67: With your sword-like grip lead him down like a sword cut.

Figure 68: An immobilisation for Yonkkyo.

8 Gokkyo

This is similar to ikkyo and commonly used for knife attacks. Start as for ikkyo but take uke's wrist from underneath not on top.

Technique 69, enter deeply as for ikkyo.
Figure 70: Gokkyo – right hand takes underneath.

Figure 71: An immobilisation for Gokkyo.

Figure 72: An alternative immobilisation.

9 Irimi nage

Begin your movement with exercise 10, then as you start to tai sabaki behind uke take the neck with a clingy hand. Continue your movement and using both hands lead uke down to your shoulder. As he reaches you, change your direction and go through with your hip.

His head and neck may be entrapped by your arm, at an angle as he reaches you and this will keep him off posture. Use your hip to throw not the arm. As your hip turns and goes through it will go down and uke with it. He should be absorbed so that his legs continue to move forwards as his top half is stopped and thrown back.

A common mistake is to let uke turn on the spot so that he is still on posture while you have to move around him. Although you are going a tai sabaki you must make him move around you by coordinating your movements and leading.

Another common mistake is to release the hand on the back of the neck completely so that uke can drift away. If you release the neck keep this hand somewhere on the body so that you still have control. You could also start this technique with exercise 6. Change direction as you release his grip. Alternatively you could start by exercise 9, again releasing his hold and changing direction as he approaches. Do not forget that you will always need to control.

Figure 51: Enter deeply as in exercise 8.

Figure 52: Lead Uke around you.

Figure 75: Your arm should be ready to meet his movement.

Figure 76: Uke falls as your hip turns and goes through.

10 Kaitennage

This is a fascinating throw – a rotary throw. At the moment of projection, uke's body has to be turned and tilted so that one shoulder is leading downwards into the tatami.

Figure 77: Enter as in exercise 10.

Figure 78: Keep Uke's body turning.

Start by exercise 10. As you tai sabaki to the side and behind him, the circular movement of his arm should continue to control his body and lead him into the correct position.

Remember that the movement of your centre is going to achieve this, not the movement of your arms. Coordination is all important. If you are reaching with your arms then you have not coordinated them with your body.

As his body is being turned with your tai sabaki, use your free arm to make contact with his pinned arm and continue the movement. If this is a nice circular movement you will find that your other hand (the one which was originally taken and which was released as you moved), may come to rest on the back of his neck. With both hands continue leading him to your centre, then change direction and go forwards with your hip. As you do this the hand holding his arm will go forward with the same hip. Your hand should not go in the gap between his arm and body. This would be OK for a hiji jime or sumiotoshi but not for kaitennage.

Don't reach for the neck or pull it. Everything should always fall into place. Both hands should act together and be coordinated with the body. With Kaitennage a common mistake is to crowd yourself so that you haven't room to move and then you try to do everything with your arms. It ends as a fight.

You can also start the kaitennage in the same way that I mentioned for Ikkyo. Once under the arch made by his arm, turn and continue as above. This way he must be taken off posture by forming the arch and kept off posture during your movement.

Figure 79: Absorb his movement, still turning.   *Figure 80: Use hips to turn his body to your centre.*   *Figure 81: Left arm and hip work together, leg follows.*

Chapter 4

BASIC PRINCIPLES

One of the basic principles of Aikido is relaxation. This may not seem easy especially when held tightly by one or more people but it is something which must be practised and learned. When you are tense you give out aggression and your opponent feels this and reacts to your every move. Relax and he feels nothing. he has nothing to fight. In this way you can continue your movements without barriers.

The Japanese have a saying "yu yoku go o seisu". Soft and flexible equates with life and vitality, hard and stiff with withering and death. Think of a good solid tree. When the storms come if it cannot give with the wind, it will be uprooted and die. What of the weed that forces its way up through the concrete of a drive. Even gentle streams make their way through stone beds in their own time. Relaxation helps your natural power flow. Tension not only stops the flow of power but can also injure the body.

Some years ago, at a local club, there were two strong, well built men who practised Aikido but who were competitive. Each considered the other his rival. let us call them Steve and Dave. There was little cooperation between them and they were always determined to prevent the other from completing a movement or throw. The instructor told them that they should be flexible in body and mind and that they like the solid trees still had to give way to natural power. One day the inevitable happened. Despite his best efforts to keep on his feet, Steve was thrown with movement power. His body was so rigid that the shock to his system caused a blood clot in the main artery leading to the brain. He eventually recovered in hospital.

So relaxation is important whether you are attacking or defending. A weak attack, however, requires more skill on the part of the defender. A good strong attack enables your partner (tori) to practise his technique. If your body is stiff and rigid, when you attack, you will be unable to use natural power and you will not be able to respond so quickly and easily if it is necessary to breakfall. Look around and you will see that generally people attack as they defend. This should be with spirit and natural power.

Good strong posture is essential. You must stand firmly but not rigidly. Good posture does not mean "posturing", i.e. standing ready in a stance showing one and all that you are ready for a fight. It means keeping your weight central so that you can move in any given direction without losing your balance. Beginners frequently forget that they have legs because they are static. They lose posture because they reach instead of moving their centre.

Impatience in the execution of a technique will upset posture. You will lean when you try to reach something instead of moving into the correct position. Everything should fall into place when you are doing the right thing at the right time in the right place. Looking down or focusing on some object, i.e. a hand or a foot can also throw you off posture as well as stopping the flow of movement.

Musashi advises us that "The gaze should be large and broad. This is the twofold gaze "perception and sight". Perception is strong and sight weak." This is so that you can perceive the whole picture, keeping alert and on posture, without being distracted by insignificant movements.

Movement does not mean moving to one spot and remaining there. Movement is flowing and continuous. It stretches to infinity. So often we think that we have completed our movement when we have failed to do technique. The truth is that we did not finish the movement. We should have gone yet further. With an irimi technique (entering), it is useful to look beyond your opponent and go through him. With a tenkan movement make sure that you have turned fully. Above all practice exercises like tai sabaki so that movement is relaxed, natural and complete.

Remember the heavy wheelbarrow being pushed up the hill? If it stops, you'll never get it started again. If you continue you can build up momentum and the wheelbarrow steams down the other side of the hill. I have also been told that you should start like a gentle breeze and finish like a tornado. This is impossible to do if you are thinking what you are doing at the same time. Like the irimi thoughts should be already beyond what you are doing.

Again if we imagine the natural movements of the sea, the waves roll in and out again. Their movements flow in a circular path and they rise and fall. Our movements should imitate them.

Control of yourself and of your opponent must be maintained throughout your movement. If you do not control your mind, thoughts will interfere with your movement and your movement will cease to flow. If you do not control your body, you will not be in the right place at the right time doing the right thing. Physical training is there to rid us of physical habits which holds back, i.e. leaning, stepping out, reaching. Training in Budo helps us get rid of bad mental habits which inhibit us, i.e. fear, impatience. Both types of training, mental and physical, should go side by side and be complementary.

When we control our pride and ego, we can accept criticism and learn. Impatience, resentment and jealousy may arise when the mind is not controlled. They naturally lead to errors of judgement in Aikido and in life. The most timid ladies, who have come to me for self defence training, become confident and positive beyond all recognition through practice. Cure reaching on the tatami and you will be more content to wait for other things. Practise Budo and Aikido and the benefits will emerge in your everyday life also.

As in life, if you do not control your opponent, he will control you. You must take him off posture and maintain this advantage. He must be lead where you want him to go and held when you want him in one place. Make sure that you move him around you rather than running around him. In many sports like squash, he who controls the best position in the court, controls the game. In Aikido too ensure that you have the advantage, i.e. as soon as he attacks, take control. I have seen experienced Aikidoka take control even before he has attacked, by their bearing, mental attitude and their initial movement.

The other basics are coordination and synchronisation of movement. You must coordinate your movements with that of your attacker so that you can avoid the attack or absorb it. To absorb, deflect and project, your movements must be synchronised, i.e. hands, arms, hips centre must be working like clockwork. Good timing is important in any attack and takes a lot of practice. Musashi's "broad gaze" helps if you see the whole person rather than waiting for his arm to lift for the attack.

The distance that you should maintain from an opponent (Maai), depends on your own stature and that of your opponent. You will find your maai with the help of your instructor. With the incorrect maai, you may find it impossible to coordinate with the attack.

These are the basics which are learned in many years practice of peaceful Aikido, the Art. Other principles and refinements are also accumulated by the keen practitioner. Practical Aikido used for the purposes of self defence is more direct and the importance of particular aspects takes on a different emphasis.

For example, when it is a question of self preservation the emphasis is jointly on posture and movement. If you can tai sabaki out of an attack or escape from a hold, this is also Aikido. Consider the saying, "My enemy stands before me, sword drawn. But I am no longer there, I now stand behind him!" Not only have you avoided the attack but you have gained control of the situation.

Jo against Jo sequence.

Chapter 5

BUKI (WEAPONRY)

Prince Tejuin of the Minamoto family is credited with founding Aiki Jujitsu in the ninth century. His descendan t Shinra Saburo improved this system further and called it Daito-ryu Aiki-jujitsu. These systems were the predecessors of modern Aikido. Both of them primarily taught weapons and supplemented this teaching with empty-handed techniques. Only when you start to train with weapons will you start to see the proper flow of movement necessary for good Aikido.

The sword (ken) is the most popular weapon of the samurai. The sword is the samurai's soul as such, honoured and revered. Only the samurai were allowed to wear two swords. Wooden swords called bokken were often used in practice and could be as lethal as real ones. Later bamboo was used to create the shinai now used in Kendo.

Another popular weapon was the lance or naginata. There would often be great debates over which was the best weapon. In Japan, women still train with naginata but in the west we train with the nearest equivalents, the bo or jo. These are eight foot or six foot staffs. These are fascinating weapons giving great flexibility of movement. According to the story of Musashi, the great swordsman of the 17th century, who was never defeated with the sword he lost a fight against a man with a jo, stopping the fight before he was killed.

Knife or Tanto techniques are also basic to Aikido. Samurai women were given knives to conceal about their person in case of attack. They knew exactly how to use the knife on their own throats to preserve their honour and dignity. Self defence against knife is however more relevant to us and our training.

Whatever weapon we use it is important that we use it with flexibility. You must blend your movement and that of the weapon. This is not just the movement of your hands but body movement – the movement of your centre to make a blow

Jo against Sword sequence.

more powerful or to move into a position where you will have the advantage or be more powerful.

To hold a weapon properly do not grip but hold with a clingy feel. In the Book of Five Rings Mushai says, "Grip the long sword with a floating feeling in your thumb and forefinger, with the middle finger neither tight nor slack and with the last two fingers tight. It is bad to have play in your hands." This is the classic grip for sword or for sankkyo, yonkko or any other hold. He goes on, "Generally I dislike fixedness in both long swords and hands. Fixedness means a dead man."

Beginners in Aikido are always rigid. They stand with shoulders square and refuse to use their hips. The leg moves forward but not the centre. Everything is on one level. It is impossible to draw a sword without also moving the hips. A turning movement releases the sword and lets it fly from the scabbard. A lowering movement adds to the power of this release. If sword cuts are performed with shoulders and arms instead of the centre, the arms soon begin to ache. This is wrong. Wrists, on he other hand will ache. They are needed for the cutting action and to control the movement of the sword.

In this way, practice with your sword will lead you into good practice in empty-handed Aikido. It will lead to good posture, stability and the use of hips and centre. It will also encourage you to use different levels of movement and make wrists more flexible. This also applies in reverse. Practise diligently the principles of Aikido and you will find the sword.

In the West we do not often practice with lance or naginata. The modern equivalents are bo or jo. A bo is staff, approximately six foot long. The jo is about four-and-a-half foot. Both weapons are amazingly versatile. They can be used to obtain a pin, to control or to atemi (strike). In particular, any aggression is transmitted through the jo so it must be used in a relaxed but positive manner. Most techniques that can be performed with empty hands may also be performed with the jo.

Imagine if the centre of the jo is the fulcrum, one end of the jo will manipulate the other. If the fulcrum of the jo is moved, different sized circles will be created. When your centre moves these become ellipses. Your opponent may be moved through any of these paths.

The hanto and hanbo are like clubs or sticks. They may be used to atemi, to control or to take an opponent off posture. They may also be used to make circular movements which lead the opponent where you want him. As with all weapons you should know how to use them, but not rely on them.

As well as promoting the correct movements and holds, the use of weapons makes us more used to facing danger and more oblivious to fear In everyday life some people feel more worried about going to the dentist, to the hospital or taking an examination than others. No matter how timid they are, after facing a sword or an attack with the jo say in yokomen (sidewards blow), a visit to the dentist fades into significance.

A couple of years ago, a friend was returning from a nightclub with is wife and two other friends on the motorway. A car repeatedly passed them and then braked in front of them until they were forced into a layby. A big hulking man descended from the car brandishing a large staff. He was obviously enjoying the look of terror on some of their faces. My friend, however, had been practising jo work recently and knew what to do. He told the brute exactly where he was going to stick it. (I'm not sure if there is a name for this technique). The brute very rapidly took to his car and vanished.

I think that this is an example of the "Fudo-shin " so important in Budo. It is gratifying to know that we can develop and progress in this way. Fudo-shin is something like unshakable or firm heart. When asked about this Musashi answered, "There is a long wooden board here (it was 10 cm wide). Can you walk on it? Yes you can walk on it. It is easy. Next, if the board is at 2 metres height, can you walk on it? Yes you may well be able to walk on it. Then, if the board lies between two mountains a hundred metres high or more, can you walk on it? Well, that is Fudo-shin."

When adults or children have learned tai sabaki I have sometimes tested them by attacking with a bokken from shomen (a cut straight down to the head). Now they must not dodge the blow or duck. They have to keep their nerve and move correctly. Soon they build up the confidence to maintain posture, and tai sabaki even when the attack is much faster.

Tanto waza or tanto tori (knife techniques or knife taking), bring another dimension to the practice of Aikido. You may be competent at kote gaeshi from tsuki but fear uke now that he is using a knife. It should make no difference. Never try to take the blade, instead you must stop the man from using the blade. It is no danger without him. Musashi in the Book of Five Rings says that your eyes should not be fixed on the enemies' sword as your spirit may become confused and your strategy thwarted. It is just the same with the knife blade. Musashi continues: "As I said before if you fix your eyes on details and neglect important things, your spirit will become bewildered and victory will escape you."

Knife attack; defend using Irimi.

Figure 1: The Sword is drawn and ready.

Figures 2, 3: The Sword cuts shomen.

Figures 4, 5: Kesa-giri.

73

Figures 1, 2: Offering the Jo.

Figures 3, 4: Nikkyo using a Jo.

Figures 1, 2, 3: Irimi nage using a Jo.

Figures 1–3: Ikkyo using a Jo.

Figures 1–4: Shiho nage using a Hanbo.

Other weapons may be studied but in a flexible manner. Trevor Leggett in "The Spirit of Budo" tells of a martial arts display that he once attended where a particular school gave a display on the use of saucepan lids. They only trained with these weapons. He was quite surprised and asked for the origins of this art. He was told that a master of martial arts once told his pupils to attack him at any time to sharpen further his zanshin. Once caught in the kitchen he reached for the closest utensils to be used in his defence – two saucepan lids. His pupils sadly misunderstood and thought that this was the only way to defend themselves. He tried to show adaptability and flexibility but they failed to understand.

At one time practice with weapons was frowned upon by a lot of clubs until you reached a certain dan grade. In the fifties and sixties, Pat Stratford visited many clubs on the continent seeking good Aikido before he found what he was looking for in Norio Tao and Master Tanaka. He learned what he could from various different masters, going for years without a grading. On more than one occasion he was told that he could not use a jo as he was not a dan grade. However he was not a man to listen to such nonsense and he proceeded to send black belts and all flying. Weapons training is useful and interesting to all grades of Aikidoka benefiting both Aikido practise and personal lives.

This is simply an introduction to the use of weapons in Aikido. The basic principles remain the same because Aikido was originally based upon weapons training. Practise with weapons and become comfortable with them but never complacent.

Chapter 6

FINAL STEPS

How many people would travel along a road if they did not know where it was leading? I, for one, am enjoying the journey so much that at times I think that the destination does not matter. If perfection in Aikido can never be achieved, how do we know our goal and where does our inspiration come from?

I have video tapes of Master Tanaka, which show the power and beauty of Aikido. Although I appreciate what is there, I do not pretend to understand all that is shown. Video tapes may however be misleading to beginners as you have to be able to work out what exactly is going on. This is difficult enough when it is taking place before you on a tatami. Your own instructor may provide your inspiration. If he is good, he will develop and improve as you yourself progress so that you never reach his level.

However, the achievement of perfect technique is not all that we are talking about here. A beginner moves as he is told and does not know technique. A Master knows technique but he is not tied to the constraints of technique. He has the movement, posture, coordination, synchronisation and the power to go beyond them. He also has the spirit and the void.

To understand these things we must study the principles of Budo and in particular understand the Japanese meanings of the Heart, the Spirit and the Void.

Our minds are often cluttered with worries, with thoughts about what we have to do, or things that we want. In this state our minds are not free and it is difficult to find solutions. There is no void.

Even when we know what we want to do, we often do not get past the stage of "yes, I would like to do that". How many people say that they would love to do Aikido but never turn up? Thoughts are not translated into action. Perhaps the idea satisfied the ego but there was no substance to the thought. There was no heart and no spirit.

Miyamoto Musashi.

The mind must be free to act without intrusion of thoughts, to accept what must be without regrets – non aggression and non resistance. This is the void.

In the book of the void (Musashi's Five Rings), it states "nothing is the void and the void is nothingness." Yet the void is not a vacuum. It is a space through which sounds, objects or knowledge may pass to be stored in memory banks or to give rise to actions. The space is never cluttered so that it is always free to receive input. There is nothing to obstruct the learning processes or to hinder actions.

We must have the heart to practise and study despite all difficulties. If our minds are free and our hearts are strong then there are no obstacles. Obstacles only exist when our minds put them there. Inability to perform a technique is not an obstacle, it is a temporary setback. When we have the necessary, wisdom and knowledge and skill we will succeed. If we have the heart to continue practising, these things will come to us in time. Patience and hard work win through not impatience and wanting.

The true spirit of movement is to be powerful without aggression and to flow without obstacles. Nature is a truly powerful force, yet there is no aggression and it heeds no obstacles. Tides ebb and flow altering coast lines. Winds blow and without will shape the trees in their path. Rivers force gullys through rock. The spirit of Budo is to flow with nature. To be insincere or to lose faith is to be without spirit.

When we have perfected physical skills, our bodies will be robust and healthy. We will be adroit and be able to defend ourselves. We will be strong in posture and positive in actions. Spiritual perfection includes self discipline and self control, self denial, devotion to universal human values, faithfulness to one's self and to others.

Following the way that I have set out in this book and practising in a dedicated manner, the first changes you will notice in yourself or in others are physical ones – improved coordination, posture and fitness. Later you may notice psychological changes – more self assurance and a more positive outlook on life. The spiritual changes will only come to those who recognise the relationship between Zen, Confucianism, Budo and Aikido and study to achieve satori (enlightenment).

In the beginning there was not the word but the mind. Zen takes us back to this state, which preceded thoughts and worldly desires. "If you have lost your true self, all phenomena will bring you nothing but annoyance. If you discover your essence of mind, you can follow nothing but the true path." This was written by Hojo Tokiyori.

Mounted Samurai with sword and bow.

There are no prayers in Zen. Since everything is cause and effect we must rely on ourselves and accept the natural consequences of our actions. If you are resentful or jealous because a fellow student has achieved a higher grade, is it not because you have not worked so hard or have less natural ability. Are you upset because you expected a grading (or a birthday present or a rise)? Is this not your own fault for expecting it? You broke an ornament. What bad luck! But wasn't it your own fault for being clumsy or careless? The more we accept this the more contented we can become.

In the "Unfettered Mind", the writings of the Zen Master, Takuan Soho to the Sword Master, says that desires arise from all the senses and from but a single thought. Briefly, desire leads to preference and to discrimination of beauty over ugliness, good over evil or pleasure over pain. "Within this body solidified by desire is concealed the absolutely desireless and upright core of mind . . . It is unwaveringly correct, it is absolutely straight. When this mind is used as a plumbline, anything done at all will be rightmindedness."

At another point he talks about a scarecrow in the mountain fields. It is fashioned into the shape of a human figure and a bow and arrow are placed into its hands. Although the creature has no mind, the deer are frightened and run away. It has served its function well. He says that this is an example of people who have reached any depths of the Way. "While hands, feet and body may move, the mind does not stop any place at all and one does not know where it is. Being in the state of No-Thought, No-Mind, one has reached the level of the scarecrow."

An interesting story illustrating this state of mind was told by Trevor Leggott in "The Spirit of budo". A Master of Kyudo, Japanese archery was offered some tips by a western style archer as it was well known that the western style bow was more accurate. The Master if Kyudo was forced to make clear why other aspects were more important than accuracy. He suggested that the western archer stand with his bow at the opposite end of the practice area. They would then stand and aim for each other. understandably, the westerner did not want to do this. He did not have the mind or the mental training.

"Zen Inklings" is a collection of stories and fables by Donald Richie, which may help you to realise more about satori. I find particularly amusing a story about a trainee monk who meditates and deprives himself of all pleasure in his search for satori. Eventually he loses faith, leaves the monastery and finds himself in the pleasure quarters of the town. During intimate moments with a prostitute, his mind is on the creaking bed, the meaning of life, his reasons for being there etc. At the moment of climax, his mind finally empties of thought and he achieves satori. When he returns to the monastery, he is questioned by his abbot and made a priest. He is given a formal new name but his parishioners prefer to call him Bobo Roshi, a name which recalls what he was doing at his moment of truth.

This story may seem irrelevant to Aikido but I can think of many Aikidoka who take their training so seriously that enjoyment never comes into it and in all likelihood neither will satori!

Inazo Nitobe in "Bushido, the Soul of Japan", mentions that the teachings of Confucius were the most prolific source of Bushido. His thoughts on the moral relationships between master and servant, father and son, husband and wife, older and younger brother and between friends were readily accepted by the Japanese people as right and proper.

Shinto doctrines already preached filial piety and reverence for ancestors, patriotism and loyalty. Confucius added more moral guidelines on rectitude, courage, benevolence, courtesy, sincerity, honour, loyalty and education. Zen, Confucianism and Shinto (the way of the Gods) have been developed by the Japanese into the concept of Bushido or Budo.

The harmony of Budo or Aikido should be enacted in everyday life. Respect the five elements – earth ,wind, fire, water and the void. We will never master them so we must work with them. So it is with people also. The story of Miyamoto Musashi was written by Eiji Yoshikawa in around 1935. Although an exciting work of fiction reconstructing the life of this famous swordsman, it deals with the principles of Budo and the way to satori.

Musashi was a strongwilled and bloodthirsty youth, who ran off to do battle at Sekigahara. Although his spirit was little more than that of a wild animal, a wise priest called Takuan took pity on him and started him on the correct path to wisdom and satori. The book follows him on this path and I think that some of the things that he begins to realise on the way, illustrate what I have been saying. Musashi has two young students/servants. The first is Jotaro, a boisterous and mischievous lad, who is spoiled by Musashi. When Jotaro is separated from Musashi, he takes on an orphan called Iori. Iori is also spirited but Musashi admonishes him, "When people live together in harmony, the earth is a paradise. But every man has a bad side as well as a good side. There are times when only the bad comes out. Then the world's not paradise but hell. There's a reason we have manners and etiquette. They keep us from letting the bad side take over. This promotes social order which is the objective of the governments laws."

Musashi decides to run a farm to do a different study. After a while, he realises: "What a fool I've been. I tried to make the water flow where I thought it should be and force the dirt to stay where I thought it should be. But it didn't work. How could it? Water's water, Dirt's dirt. I can't change their nature. What I've got to do is be a servant to the water and a protector of the dirt. The same rules must apply to governing people. Do not attempt to oppose the way of the universe. But first make sure you know the way of the universe."

Aikido and Budo teach us the Way of the Universe. We certainly have a long journey to make. Let us make it a good one.

Author instructing.

Chapter 7

TERMINOLOGY AND GLOSSARY OF TERMS

You should not worry about the Japanese terminology involved in Aikido. You will gradually increase your vocabulary and knowledge of Japanese terminology as you practice Aikido and as you learn more about Japanese ways, Aikido, Budo and Zen.

The pronunciation of Japanese is simple if not easy. Vowels are always pronounced in the same way:

a as in bat
e as in bet
i as in beat but clipped short
o as in tot
u as in hut

These vowels are very crisp and short. Vowels with a line above them are pronounced for double the length. Two vowels together for example, ae, as in kote gaeshi are pronounced individually as above. They do not form a different sound as in the English maize or mean.

Consonants are similar to those in English with the following exceptions:

g a hard sound as in goon but not soft as in gentle
f between the English f and h
r pronounced softly almost like an l

Double consonants like the ss in nissa or the pp in nippon are pronounced twice.

Equal stress is given to each syllable of a word and each is pronounced crisply.

Glossary of terms

Ai	harmony, union
Aiki taiso	exercises
Aikido	the way of spirit and harmony
Atemi awaza	the art of striking vital points
Awase	blending movements
bo	staff
bokken	wooden sword
Budo	the way of the warrior
buki	attacking with weapons
Bushi	samurai, warrior
chudan	middle
dojo	training hall
dogi	suit for training in Budo
gedan	low
gi	suit for training in Budo
gyaku	opposite
hakama	black or navy shirtlike formal wear
harmi	stance
hanmi han tachi	one standing, one kneeling techniques
hara	centre or abdomen
hidari kiki no	be left-handed
hidari	left hand
hiji waza	elbow techniques
irimi	entering, going through
irimi tsuke	entering thrust
jodan	high
jo tori	staff/stick taking
jo waza	staff/stick techniques
jujitsu	the art of gentleness of body and mind
ki	spirit, energetic power
kiai	shout, yell
Kami	deity
Kansetsu waza	the art of holding, controlling limbs
kata	shoulder or form (form of movements)
Katana	sword
katame waza	immobilisation techniques
Kawashi waza	the art of avoiding, dodging and deflecting
kogeiki	assault, attack
kokyu	breath (like ki)

maai	distance
men	head, face
migite	right hand
migikiki no	be right-handed
mochi	hold
nage waza	the art of throwing
o uchi	inside, under
o soto	outside
rei	bow of respect
riai	reason, logic
satori	enlightenment, realisation
seiza	formal sitting
shikko	knee walking
sumi	corner
suwari waza	kneeling/sitting techniques
tanto waza	knife techniques
tatami	mat
tenkan	bypass to avoid a force
tome waza	the art of blocking
tori	person executing a technique
uchi	strike
uchitachi	attacker with sword
uketachi	defender from sword
uke	one who is lead or thrown
ukemi	breakfall, taking a fall
yari	spear
yoko	side
waza	technique
zanshin	awareness of mind
zazen	seated zen meditation
Zen	Zen buddhism

Attacks

Attacks in Budo can be classified as follows:

(1) Tori and Shime	holding and strangle hold
(2) Uchi	hitting and cutting
(3) Tsuki	striking and punching
(4) Keri	kicking
(5) Buki	attacking with weapons

Judo specialises in attacks as in no. 1.
Kendo specialises in attacks 2, 3 and 5.
Karate specialises in attacks 3 and 4.
Aikido deal with all these attacks.

Defence may be classified as follows:

(l) Kawashi waza and tome waza	the arts of dodging and blocking
(2) Osae waza and shime waza	the arts of holding down and strangling
(3) Kansetsu waza	the arts of bending and twisting joints
(4) Nage waza	the art of throwing
(5) Atemi waza	the art of striking vital points

The Judoka learns defences as in 1, 2 and 4.
the Kendoist learns defences as in 1 and 5.
The Karateka learns defences 1, 3 and 5.
The Aikidoka learns 1, 2, 3, 4 and 5.

You may hear the following terms used for attacks in Aikido.

Buki	attacking with weapons
Eri tori	collar take
Gyaku katate tori	one-handed attack, right to right etc.
Kamae	bodily attitude
Kata tori	shoulder take
Katate tori	left hand takes right hand or vice versa
keri	kicking
Hiji tori	elbow take
Mochi	grip
Mune tori	lapel hold
Shomen or shomen uchi	strike downwards to the head
Shomen kubi shime	Strangle from the front
Tori	take, hold or one who applies technique
Tsuki	hitting or thrusting
Uchi	hitting and cutting
Ushiro dakishime	bearhug from behind
Ushiro kubi shime	strangle from behind
Ushiro ryote tori	both hands taken from behind
Ushiro ryote tori kubi shime	attack from behind, one around the neck, the other holding the arm
Yokomen or yokomen uchi	side blow
Yoko kubi shime	strangle from the side

Basic techniques

The first ten techniques are the best known and most widely taught to kyu grades. they are included in Chapter 4.

Shihonage	4 ways throw
Tenchi nage	heaven and earth
Kote gaeshi	wrist throw
Ikkyo	Arm pin
Nikkyo	wrist control
Irimi nage	Entering throw
Sankkyo	control of wrist and arm
Yonkkyo	control of wrist and arm
Gokkyo	control of wrist and arm
Kalten nage	rotary throw
Kokyu nage	breath throw
Sumiotoshi	corner drop
Aiki nage	aiki throw
Koshi nage	hip throw
Hiji jime/hiji shime	elbow lock
Juji garami	cross twine throw
Tenbin nage	corner throw

Acknowledgements

Thanks to Pat Stratford, National Coach of the Aikido Union of England, for the checks on the accuracy of technical information and for his teaching. For information about classes throughout the UK, his address is Wyken Croft Community Centre, Wyken Croft, Coventry. Tel: 01203 617363.

Thanks to Norio Tao and Master Shigeho Tanaka for guidance, encouragement and inspiration. Address: Shiseikan Doji Meiji Jingu, Tokyo.

The following books have influenced my thinking and are sometimes referred to in the text:
Zen Inklings, Donald Richie, Weatherhill Press.
Japanese Tales and Legends, retold by Helen and William McAlpine, Oxford University Press.
The Spirit of Budo, Trevor Leggott.
A Book of Five Rings, Myamoto Mushashi.
Bushido, The Soul of Japan, Inazo Nitobe, Charles E. Tuttle & Co. Publishers.

The Unfettered Mind, Takuan Soho, translated by William Scott Wilson, Kodansha International.
The Book of the Samurai, Stephen Turnbull, Magna Books.
Miyamoto Mushashi, Eiji Yoshikawa, Kodansha International.